A WORLD OF WORDS

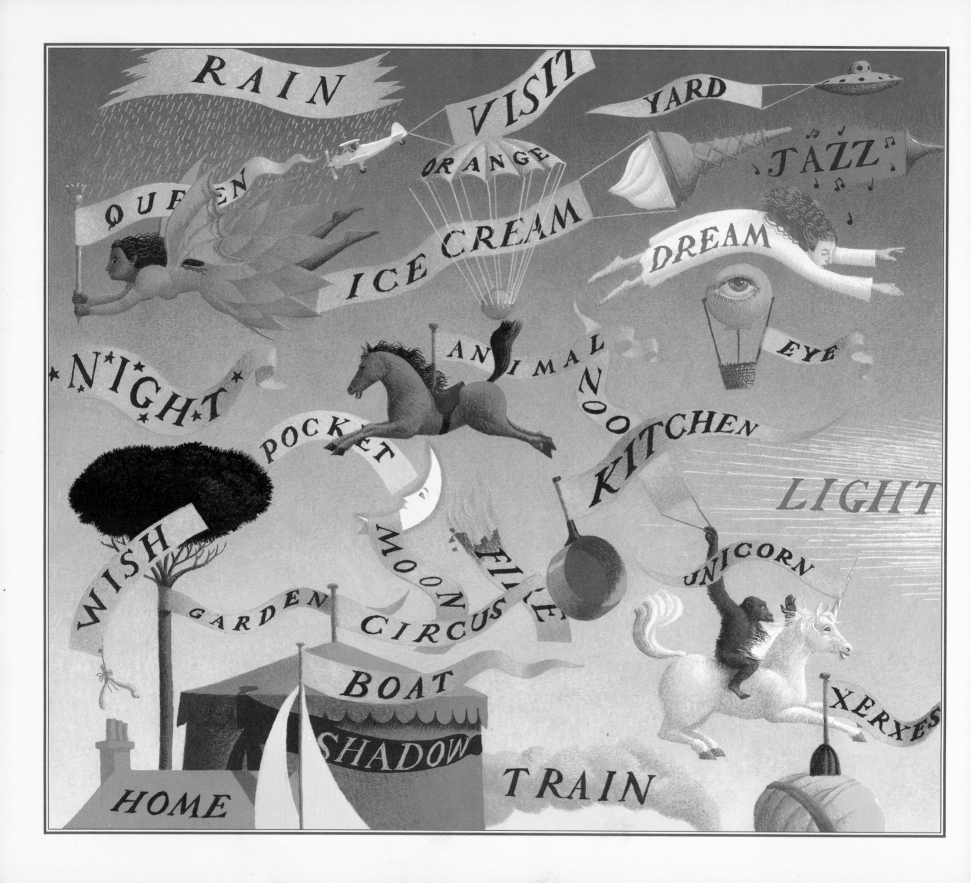

A WORLD OF WORDS

AN ABC OF QUOTATIONS

TOBI TOBIAS

ILLUSTRATED BY PETER MALONE

LOTHROP, LEE & SHEPARD BOOKS · MORROW

NEW YORK

For Renée J. Kohn, who has a way with words

—T.T.

From P. to P. who sits in B.
and long since learnt her ABC

—P.M.

The word is the making of the world.   —Wallace Stevens

Animal

In the very earliest time
when both people and animals lived on earth,
a person could become an animal if he wanted to
and an animal could become a human being. . . .
All spoke the same language.   —Inuit Eskimo

Book

As a child, I had two copies of each of my favorite books:
one for the bathtub, and one for dry land.   —Kate Guess

I cannot live without books.   —Thomas Jefferson

I always wanted to write books, ever since I found out that
it was people who wrote them.   —M. B. Goffstein

Circus

when god decided to invent
everything he took one
breath bigger than a circustent
and everything began   —e e cummings

Dream

"Why ever did I wake up!" he cried.
"I was having such beautiful dreams."
— J. R. R. Tolkien

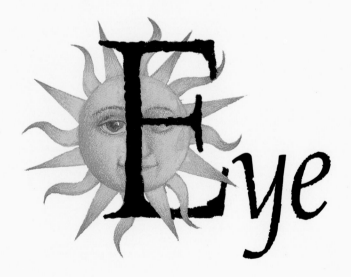

Eye

My eyes make pictures, when they are shut.
— Samuel Taylor Coleridge

Fire

Youk'n hide de fier, but w'at you gwine do wid de smoke?

—Joel Chandler Harris

Garden

I listened from a beach-chair in the shade
To all the noises that my garden made. —W. H. Auden

Home

All around me quiet.
All around me peaceful.
All around me lasting.
All around me home. —Ute Indian

# Ice Cream

The only emperor is the emperor of ice-cream.   —Wallace Stevens

If it don't melt all will be well, otherwise all won't—
don't melt, ice-cream, don't melt, I esk you like a brudda—
don't melt, ice-cream, dahlink, not yet not yet.   —George Herriman

Jazz

Drum on your drums, batter on your banjoes,
sob on the long cool winding saxophones.
Go to it, O jazzmen. —Carl Sandburg

Kitchen

my mama has made bread
and grampaw has come
and everybody is drunk
and dancing in the kitchen
and singing in the kitchen
oh these is good times
good times
good times

oh children think about the
good times —Lucille Clifton

Light

Let there be light. —Book of Genesis

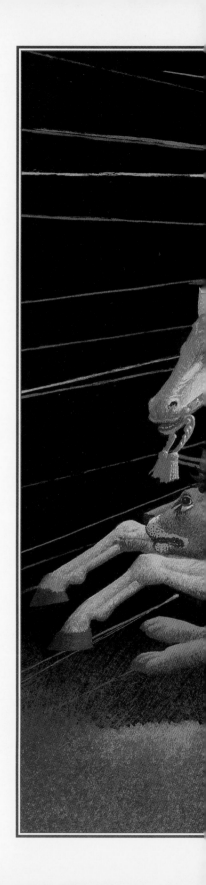

Moon

The moon, like a flower
In heaven's high bower,
With silent delight
Sits and smiles on the night.   —William Blake

Night

That is my dream! . . .
To fling my arms wide
In the face of the sun,
Dance! Whirl! Whirl!
Till the quick day is done.
Rest at pale evening . . .
A tall, slim tree . . .
Night coming tenderly
  Black like me.   —Langston Hughes

range

I peeled my orange
That was so bright against
The gray of December
That, from some distance,
Someone might have thought
I was making a fire in my hands. — Gary Soto

ocket

You love me so much, you want to put me in your pocket.
— D. H. Lawrence

Queen

You spotted snakes with double tongue,
Thorny hedgehogs, be not seen;
Newts and blind-worms, do no wrong,
Come not near our fairy queen.

—William Shakespeare

ain

Oh, the rain comes a pitter, patter,
And I'd like to be safe in bed.
Skies are weeping
While the world is sleeping
Trouble heaping
On our head.
It is vain to remain and chatter,
And to wait for a clearer sky;
Helter-skelter I must fly for shelter
Till the clouds roll by.

—Jerome Kern and P. G. Wodehouse

Shadow

A shadow his father makes with joined hands
And thumbs and fingers nibbles on the wall
Like a rabbit's head.   —Seamus Heaney

And this I have learned—
grownups do not know the language of shadows.

—Opal Whiteley

Train

There isn't a train I wouldn't take,
No matter where it's going.   —Edna St. Vincent Millay

Unicorn

"Well, now that we *have* seen each other," said the Unicorn,
"if you'll believe in me, I'll believe in you. Is that a bargain?"
"Yes, if you like," said Alice.   —Lewis Carroll

Visit

Oh, do not ask, "What is it?"
Let us go and make our visit.   —T. S. Eliot

Wish

with a swoop and a dart
out flew his wish
(it dived like a fish
but it climbed like a dream)
throbbing like a heart
singing like a flame   —e e cummings

Xerxes

X was King Xerxes,
Who wore on his head
A mighty large turban,
Green, yellow, and red.   —Edward Lear

 **Yard**

I want . . . I want a ship from some near star
To land in the yard.   —Randall Jarrell

human wandering through the zoo
what do your cousins think of you   —Don Marquis

Gouache was used for the full-color illustrations.
The text type is 16-point Carolina.

Collection copyright © 1998 by Tobi Tobias
Illustrations copyright © 1998 by Peter Malone

Published by Lothrop, Lee & Shepard Books
an imprint of Morrow Junior Books
a division of William Morrow and Company, Inc.
1350 Avenue of the Americas, New York, NY 10019
www.williammorrow.com

Printed in Singapore at Tien Wah Press.

10 9 8 7 6 5 4 3 2 1

Library of Congress Cataloging-in-Publication Data
Tobias, Tobi.
A world of words/by Tobi Tobias; illustrated by Peter Malone.
p. cm.
Summary: An alphabetical collection of poems covering a diverse range of subjects, from animals to zoos.
ISBN 0-688-12129-2 (trade) — ISBN 0-688-12130-6 (library)
1. Children's poetry, American.   2. English language—Alphabet—Juvenile literature.
[1. Poetry—Collections.   2. Alphabet.]   1. Malone, Peter, date, ill.   11. Title
PS3570.O285W67 1998   811'.54   [E]—DC20   96-16313   CIP AC

ACKNOWLEDGMENTS

Grateful acknowledgment is made to those granting permission to use material quoted in this volume.

Epigraph: "The word is..." by Wallace Stevens from "Description Without Place" in *The Collected Poems of Wallace Stevens*. Reprinted by permission of Alfred A. Knopf, Inc./Random House, Inc.

Animal: "In the very earliest time..." by an anonymous Inuit Eskimo, translated by Edward Field.

Book: "As a child..." by Kate Guess. Used by permission of the author. "I cannot live..." from a letter from Thomas Jefferson to John Adams in *The Adams-Jefferson Letters*, edited by Lester J. Cappon. Copyright 1959 by the University of North Carolina Press. Used by permission of the University of North Carolina Press. "I always wanted..." by M. B. Goffstein from "M. B. Goffstein: An Interview," by Sylvia and Kenneth Marantz, *The Horn Book Magazine*, November/December 1986. Reprinted by permission of The Horn Book, Inc., 11 Beacon Street, Suite 1000, Boston, MA 02108.

Circus: "when god decided to invent..." from "when god decided to invent" in *Complete Poems: 1904–1962*, by E. E. Cummings, edited by George J. Firmage. Copyright © 1944, 1972, 1991 by the Trustees for the E. E. Cummings Trust. Reprinted by permission of Liveright Publishing Corporation.

Dream: "Why ever did I..." from *The Hobbit*, by J. R. R. Tolkien. Copyright © 1937, 1938, and 1966 by J. R. R. Tolkien. Reprinted by permission of the Tolkien Estate.

Eye: "My eyes make pictures..." by Samuel Taylor Coleridge from "A Day-Dream" in *The Poems of Samuel Taylor Coleridge*.

Fire: "Youk'n hide de fier..." by Joel Chandler Harris from "Plantation Proverbs" in *Uncle Remus, His Songs and Sayings*, published by Penguin USA.

Garden: "I listened..." by W. H. Auden from "Their Lonely Betters" in *W. H. Auden: Collected Poems*, edited by E. Mendelson. Copyright © 1976 by Edward Mendelson, William Meredith, and Monroe K. Spears, executors of the Estate of W. H. Auden. Reprinted by permission of Random House, Inc., and Faber and Faber Limited.

Home: "All around me..." by an anonymous Ute Indian from *War Cry on a Prayer Feather: Prose and Poetry of the Ute Indians*, by Nancy Wood. Reprinted by permission of Nancy Wood.

Ice cream: "The only emperor..." by Wallace Stevens from "The Emperor of Ice Cream" in *The Collected Poems of Wallace Stevens*. Reprinted by permission of Alfred A. Knopf, Inc./Random House, Inc. "If it don't melt..." by George Herriman from *Krazy Kat: The Comic Art of George Herriman*. Reprinted by permission of James Graham & Sons.

Jazz: "Drum on your drums..." from "Jazz Fantasia" in *Smoke and Steel*, by Carl Sandburg. Copyright 1920 by Harcourt Brace & Company and renewed 1948 by Carl Sandburg. Reprinted by permission of the publisher.

Kitchen: "my mama..." from "good times" in *Good Woman: Poems and a Memoir 1969–1980*, by Lucille Clifton. Copyright © 1987 by Lucille Clifton. Reprinted by permission of BOA Editions, Ltd., 92 Park Avenue, Brockport, NY 14420.

Light: "Let there be light" from Genesis 1:3, the King James Version of the Bible.

Moon: "The moon..." from "Night" in *Songs of Innocence* by William Blake.

Night: "That is my dream!..." by Langston Hughes from "Dream Variation" in *The Collected Poems of Langston Hughes*. Copyright © 1994 by the Estate of Langston Hughes. Reprinted by permission of Alfred A. Knopf, Inc.

Orange: "I peeled my orange..." from "Oranges" in *New and Selected Poems*, by Gary Soto. Copyright © 1995 by Gary Soto. Reprinted by permission of Chronicle Books.

Pocket: "You love me so much..." from *Sons and Lovers*, by D. H. Lawrence. Copyright © the Estate of Frieda Lawrence Ravagli 1992. Reprinted by permission of Penguin USA and Laurence Pollinger Ltd. and the Estate of Frieda Lawrence Ravagli.

Queen: "You spotted snakes..." by William Shakespeare from *A Midsummer Night's Dream*.

Rain: "Oh, the rain comes..." from "Till the Clouds Roll By," written by Jerome Kern and Sir P. G. Wodehouse. Copyright © 1917 PolyGram International Publishing, Inc. Copyright renewed. Used by permission. All rights reserved.

Shadow: "A shadow..." from "Alphabets" in *The Haw Lantern*, by Seamus Heaney. Copyright © 1987 by Seamus Heaney. Reprinted by permission of Farrar, Straus & Giroux, Inc., and Faber and Faber Limited. "And this I have learned..." by Opal Whiteley from *The Story of Opal*, first published by the Atlantic Monthly Press.

Train: "There isn't a train..." from "Travel" by Edna St. Vincent Millay in *Collected Poems*, HarperCollins. Copyright 1921, 1948 by Edna St. Vincent Millay. Reprinted by permission of Elizabeth Barnett, literary executor.

Unicorn: "'Well, now that we *have* seen each other...'" from *Through the Looking-glass and What Alice Found There*, by Lewis Carroll.

Visit: "Oh, do not ask..." from "The Love Song of J. Alfred Prufrock" in *Collected Poems 1909–1962*, by T. S. Eliot. Copyright 1936 by Harcourt Brace & Company, copyright © 1964, 1963 by T. S. Eliot. Reprinted by permission of the publisher.

Wish: "with a swoop and a dart..." from "o by the by" in *Complete Poems: 1904–1962*, by E. E. Cummings, edited by George J. Firmage. Copyright © 1944, 1972, 1991 by the Trustees for the E. E. Cummings Trust. Reprinted by permission of Liveright Publishing Corporation.

Xerxes: "X was King Xerxes..." from *The Complete Nonsense Book*, by Edward Lear, edited by Lady Strachy.

Yard: "I want...I want..." from "A Sick Child" in *The Complete Poems*, by Randall Jarrell. Copyright © 1969 by Mrs. Randall Jarrell. Reprinted by permission of Farrar, Straus & Giroux, Inc., and Faber and Faber Limited.

Zoo: "human wandering..." from "archy at the zoo" in *archy and mehitabel*, by Don Marquis. Reprinted by permission of Doubleday, a division of Bantam Doubleday Dell Publishing Group, Inc.

Postscript: "A word is dead..." by Emily Dickinson, poem 1212 in *The Complete Poems of Emily Dickinson*. Reprinted by permission of Little, Brown and Company.

A word is dead
When it is said,
Some say.
I say it just
Begins to live
That day.   —Emily Dickinson